THE ELECTRIC BIBLE

THE ELECTRIC BIBLE
POEMS FOR PUBLIC WORSHIP

PETER DAINTY

kevin
mayhew

First published in 2003 by

KEVIN MAYHEW LTD
Buxhall, Stowmarket, Suffolk, IP14 3BW
E-mail: info@kevinmayhewltd.com

KINGSGATE PUBLISHING INC
1000 Pannell Street, Suite G, Columbia, MO 65201
E-mail: sales@kingsgatepublishing.com

9 8 7 6 5 4 3 2 1 0

ISBN 1 84417 041 1
Catalogue No 1500573

Cover design by Angela Selfe
Typesetting by Louise Selfe
Printed in Great Britain

To my mum and dad; long gone, but not forgotten.
They introduced me to the priceless treasure of
the Christian faith.

CONTENTS

Introduction   9

BEGINNINGS AND PATRIARCHS

Creation out of Nothing   12
God's Week   14
Let there be Light   17
In God's Image   19
Cain and Abel   21
After the Flood   23
The Tower of Babel   26
Moving On   27
Jacob   28
Joseph the Dreamer   30

PEOPLE AND PROPHETS

Middle-aged Moses   34
Burning Bush   35
At the Red Sea   37
The Ten Commandments   39
Not Bread Alone   42
Oh, that Land!   44
Clouds and Prophets   46
Chariots of Fire   48
The Prophets of God   51
One Day   53
A Prophet in Babylon   55

PSALMS AND WISDOM

Green are the Pastures   58
The Foolish Heart   59
Be Still   62
The Place of Worship   64
Sing a New Song   66
Life, Beauty and Love   67

Phoning Home   69
God Knows   70
Where can Wisdom be Found?   72
The Roundabout of Life   74
God's Good Time   77
The Candle   78

JESUS AND HIS FOLLOWERS

Superstar   80
Nunc Dimittis   82
Enough   83
The Law of Christ   85
The Lord's Prayer   87
Martha   88
Sitting by the Edge of the Pool   90
The Widow's Gift   92
King Jesus   94
Humble Access   95
Jesus Came To Save Us   96
Stones   98
Prisoner   100
In God's Garden   102
The Fruit of the Spirit   106
The Converted Church   108
North Hinksey Village Church   110
A Prayer to the Trinity   112
The Bank of Heaven   114
The Holy City   115

Scriptural Index   119

INTRODUCTION

For hundreds of years the words of the Bible have inspired people, communities and nations worldwide. The light of truth in the words of the Bible and the moral power of their teaching have fired the zeal of prophets, reformers and believers in every generation and laid the foundations of civilized life and personal faith.

The Bible has given us access to a vital moral and spiritual energy which has often, if not always, enhanced the quality of life on earth – just as electricity has given us a vital physical energy which has made possible the material benefits of the modern world.

That is why this book is called *The Electric Bible* (a sequel to *The Electric Gospel*). These poems are meant to be like plugs or switches, which will give access to the energy locked up in the familiar words of scripture by relating them to our own times and letting them throw light on contemporary issues. They are intended to be read in church in connection with passages and verses selected from the major sections of the Bible, in order to help modern Christians see something of the relevance of these ancient writings to the here and now.

Many of the poems could be divided up between several readers, or they could equally well be read by one reader only. It isn't the quantity of readers which matters, but the quality of their reading. The quality of the poems is also important, of course, and I must take full responsibility for that. I can only ask you to try them for yourself and see.

BEGINNINGS
AND
PATRIARCHS

CREATION OUT OF NOTHING

Genesis 1:1–3

Darkness is nothing
   but the absence of light;
   and, out of nothing,
   God made all things visible,
   sparking the empty black
   with blazing stars
   and innumerable mornings.

Silence is nothing
   but the absence of sound;
   and, out of nothing,
   God made all things audible,
   plucking the noiseless tension
   into the throbbing music
   of creation's song of joy.

Stillness is nothing
   but the lack of movement;
   and, out of nothing,
   God made all things move,
   broadcasting seeds of life
   in the growing fields of space.

God's nature always is
    to turn poor nothings
    into something great.
He called weak slaves
    to be his chosen nation;
    he made a dying man
    the world's salvation;
    and from the grave he raised
    a new creation.

If from such nothings
    God makes all things new,
    what might he, in his wisdom,
    make of me and you?

GOD'S WEEK

Genesis 1:1–2:3

On Sunday morning, God said,
  'Let there be Light!' –
  and there *was* Light.
'I have a vision,' he said,
  'and I need to see clearly
  to make it a reality;
  let darkness give way
  to the light of beauty,
  truth and goodness.'

On Monday morning, God said,
  'Let there be Sky!' –
  and there *was* Sky.
'I need space to work in,' he said,
  'and I want my world
  to be grand enough to be awesome,
  big enough to stretch the mind,
  and vast enough for adventure
  in the search for truth.'

On Tuesday morning, God said,
  'Let there be Land and Sea!' –
  and there *was* Land and Sea.
Then the Land produced grass
  and plants and trees
  of all kinds.
'Now the world is beginning to live,' said God.

On Wednesday morning, God said,
    'Let there be Lights in the Sky!' –
    and there *were* Lights in the Sky.
'Let the world be filled with beauty above,
    to inspire beauty below,'
    God said;
    'and let the movements
    of sun, moon and stars
    mark the passing days and seasons
    in a world of Time.'

On Thursday morning, God said,
    'Let there be Living Creatures
    in the sea and sky!' –
    and there *were* Living Creatures:
    until the oceans and the air
    were teeming with Life.

On Friday morning, God said,
    'Let the earth produce
    all kinds of animals,
    both wild and domestic;
    and the earth will nurture Life
    as long as Life nurtures the earth.'
Then God said, 'Let there be People!'
    and there *were* People.
'I need People like myself,'
    said God,
    'who can look after the world
    on my behalf.'

[Continued

On Saturday* morning,
   God said nothing.
He was resting.
But he was thinking,
   'Let there be Joy! –
   in all the order,
   the beauty,
   the life
   and the wealth
   of my creation!'

Then on Sunday morning,
   God got up again and said,
   'Let there be Light! –
   I still have a lot to do.'

* The Sabbath

LET THERE BE LIGHT

Genesis 1:3

'Let there be light,' says God,
  and his Word
  speeds through dark chaos
  on streams of fire,
  hanging the emptiness
  with spinning multitudes
  of blazing lanterns,
  until all space glows.

For God is light,
  and he must radiate
  in rising suns
  and in volcanic fire;
  in subterranean caves
  where phosphorous gleams,
  and in the darting firefly's tropic night.
Let all things shine,
  and darkness be the backcloth only
  of God's dreams.

[Continued

But that crude light we see with fleshy eyes
  is simply the beginning
  of far brighter visions.
There is a spirit-light of truth and love,
  a light displayed, not in the world of things,
  but in the human soul –
  the candle of the Lord;
  a holy radiance,
  which reveals the mystery
  of the being of God
  and lights this earth
  with heaven.

The world is not transfigured
  by our paler imitations of the sun –
  glaring electric power
  that drives the demons
  only from the surface of our minds
  to lurk in its subconscious caverns.
But we must seek that inner light,
  that pure and shadowless flame
  which leaves no hiding place
  for hate or fear.
We may dismiss it
  as the stuff of haloes
  and of angels' wings,
  but it alone can guide us
  to a dazzling destiny
  in God.

IN GOD'S IMAGE

Genesis 1:26-27

Never forget that you are made
    in the image of God.
When you are depressed by failure
    and filled with self-contempt;
    when your faith is crushed
    by cruel experience
    and you succumb to weakness
    or abuse your strength;
    never forget that you are made
    in the image of God.

Never forget
    that your neighbours are made
    in the image of God –
    including those
    who are different from you,
    who are a nuisance to you,
    who make heavy demands upon you
    and are hostile to you.
Never forget that they too are made
    in the image of God.

[Continued

And rejoice in this truth,
 that, in spite of all appearances,
 we are more than bodies and brains,
 walking chemical concoctions
 or biological computers;
 for each of us is made
 in the image of God.
And though that does not mean
 that we *are* God,
 or even that God
 is like us,
 it does mean
 there is something of God
 in us all.

CAIN AND ABEL

Genesis 4:1-16

Cain was a born loser,
   the archetypal failure,
   whose every offering
   was unacceptable,
   his efforts
   ironically fruitless.
He was the striking exception
   that proved the rule
   of God's undiscriminating mercy.
No wonder his bitter frustration
   turned to envy,
   and erupted in violence.

Abel was destined always to be right
   without really trying,
   so that his offerings
   were pleasing to God,
   and, even in death,
   his blood moved God
   to do him justice.

[Continued

But these two,
    though so different,
    were, after all, brothers;
    and we have inherited
    their traits.
When our blood is spilt
    we cry to God for vengeance,
    but when we spill the blood of others,
    we don't accept they are our brothers.

AFTER THE FLOOD

Genesis 6:5-9:17

God led Noah safely through the flood,
    from the plains of Mesopotamia
    to the mountains of Ararat.
It was a voyage between two worlds –
    from the primitive world
    of myth and legend,
    the world of gods and giants,
    into the world we know
    and now inhabit –
    the world of rules and rulers.

Eden's age of innocence
    (so the story goes)
    had given way
    to an unruly age
    of violence
    and corruption.
The Great Flood
    put an end to all that.
Afterwards,
    there was law
    based on strict justice –
    a life for a life.

[Continued

It was the beginning
   of social order and control,
   and we, the descendants of Noah,
   have inherited his world,
   although we've come a long way
   since then.

Even the animals
   were now ruled by fear.
Their flesh could be eaten,
   and their bodies offered
   in sacrifice.
Yet the eating of blood
   was forbidden,
   because the blood was the life,
   and all life was sacred.
But we've come a long way
   since then.

By the rainbow covenant
   God promised
   the stability of nature –
   enough to make possible
   the unsteady growth
   of human civilisation.
'Never again,' said God,
   'will I destroy
   all living creatures;
   and seedtime and harvest,
   cold and heat,
   summer and winter,
   day and night shall not cease
   as long as the earth endures.'
Oh glorious promise!

And we can surely trust God
    not to break that promise.
The worry now is –
    because we've come a long way
    since the days of Noah,
    can we trust *ourselves*
    not to break God's promise
    for him?

THE TOWER OF BABEL

Genesis 11:1-9

The Tower of Babel
    represents those cities
    and those empires,
    built on power and pride,
    which, stretching up
    from earth to heav'n,
    would claim
    the very throne of God.

But soon,
    beneath their weight of glory
    they divide and fall:
    their people scattered
    round the earth,
    where they are ruled
    in foreign tongues
    by others who would build
    new cities
    and yet prouder empires –
    doomed in their turn
    and left
    unfinished.

Lord, give us wisdom
    to receive at last
    that City
    which comes down from Heav'n –
    the Holy City
    filled with light and love.

MOVING ON

Genesis 12:1-9; Hebrews 11:8-10, 13-16

Abraham was called by God
> to leave his home among the nations
> and to seek a better land –
> a city that was built
> on God's foundations.

So Abraham moved on,
> not settling down
> to die in Haran
> like his father,
> but shaking off the past
> in searching for God's future.

Always travelling on
> he lived in tents,
> a stranger and a refugee
> even in Canaan;
> the father of all
> those restless
> and dissatisfied ones
> who are haunted
> by the persistent nudging
> of the living God.

Abraham's descendants
> are as countless as the stars –
> pilgrims of the spirit
> and pioneers of faith
> who are chosen, like him,
> to keep on moving on.

JACOB

Genesis 28:10-22; 32:22-32

Twice God spoke to Jacob
   in the desert night –
   once as he slept and dreamed,
   once as he fought till morning light.

Jacob the deceiver
   fled to a desert land;
   he made a rock his pillow,
   his bed was the stony sand.

But God is always with us
   wherever we may go
   and heaven is nearer than we think
   here in this world below.

He dreamed an angel ladder
   stretching to the sky
   and saw that heaven was only
   a flight of stairs away.

For God is always with us
   wherever we may go
   and heaven is nearer than we think
   here in this world below.

He woke in fear and trembling,
   completely overawed,
   and made his rocky pillow
   an altar to the Lord.

For God is always with us
   wherever we may go
   and heaven is nearer than we think
   here in this world below.

He felt that he was standing
   at heaven's very door
   and vowed to serve the Lord his God
   here on God's ground floor.

For God is always with us
   wherever we may go
   and heaven is nearer than we think
   here in this world below.

Later, when Jacob wrestled
   throughout the long dark night,
   it may have left him wounded
   but God blest him in the fight.

For God is always with us
   wherever we may go
   and heaven is nearer than we think
   here in this world below.

JOSEPH THE DREAMER

Genesis, Chapters 37, 39 to 47

Joseph, the dreamer,
    with the confidence of youth,
    believed that all his dreaming
    was the God-given truth.
His doting father dressed him
    in a robe of finest thread;
    his brothers scowled with jealousy
    and wished that he was dead.

Joseph, the dreamer,
    God is calling you.
He has plans you do not know
    to make your dreams come true.

They threw him in an empty pit
    then offered him for sale.
He became a slave in Egypt
    and ended up in jail.
Yet in spite of all his troubles,
    and the lonely path he trod,
    he clung to his integrity
    and kept his faith in God.

Joseph, the dreamer,
God is by your side.
He has plans you do not know;
he will be your guide.

Joseph, being a dreamer,
knew what secrets dreams conceal.
Vital portents of the future
he was able to reveal.
When the Pharaoh made him Governor
Joseph came to understand
his dreams were part and parcel
of the fate of Egypt's land.

Joseph, the dreamer,
God has brought you here.
He had plans you did not know;
now he makes them clear.

Joseph, Egypt's master
and dispenser of her wealth,
was raised to this high office,
to save the nation's health.
His brothers stood around him,
and begged for precious grain;
then Joseph knew his private dreams
were part of a greater aim.

Joseph, the dreamer,
God was calling you.
He had plans you did not know
until your dreams came true.

PEOPLE
AND
PROPHETS

MIDDLE-AGED MOSES

Exodus 3:1-12

Middle-aged Moses,
    hiding in the desert,
    trying to forget
    the dreams of his youth.
Once he was on fire,
    once he burned with passion;
    now he has extinguished
    the painful flame of Truth.
Sitting in the wilderness,
    married to security,
    wasting his days
    on another man's sheep;
    far from the suffering,
    far from the slavery,
    far from his brothers
    in an aimless sleep.

But then comes the burning,
    then comes the fire
    blazing in the bush –
    an inextinguishable flame.
His vision is rekindled,
    his calling reasserted
    as he rises to God's challenge
    and a never-dying fame.

BURNING BUSH

Exodus 3:2; 1 John 2:16, 17

The bush that burns and dies
    is not of God.
When its blazing turns to ashes,
    and its momentary glory
    smokes to an unsensational ending;
when today's bright star
    falls into the cold night
    of yesterday's headlines;
when the man of the hour
    withers in the heat
    of his short fame;
when the whizz-kid skids into oblivion;
when the passionate movement,
    born in fervour,
    dies of over-exposure
    in the bitter winds of change;
when the stale smell rises
    from the burnt-out fag end
    of a passing fashion;
when the bush dies with its burning,
    then you know
    that it is not of God.

[Continued

But where the bush burns
  and is not consumed,
  there is God.
Where sparks of faith
  explode in a dark age;
where martyrs' eyes
  gleam bright with hope;
where prophets' words
  shine through the mocking night;
where flames of love
  will not be quenched by hate;
where strugglers radiate joy
  and saints die on their knees;
where Christ's true light
  shines fresh in each new age;
where the bush burns
  and is not consumed,
  then you know
  that there is God.

AT THE RED SEA

Exodus 14:10-16

When the people looked behind them
    and saw Pharaoh's hosts draw near
    they turned to Moses, their leader,
    and cried out in their fear:
'We were better off in Egypt,
    we were better off as slaves,
    than buried in the desert sand
    or drowned in the Red Sea's waves.
'If freedom can offer us nothing but death,
    what is it worth?' we say.
'Let us return to the life that we knew
    in the land of yesterday.'

So Moses said to the people,
    'Stand firm, and don't be afraid;
    the Lord who has brought us this far
    will surely come to our aid.
The Egyptians you see behind you
    may look like unbeatable men,
    but when the Lord has done his work
    you'll never see them again.
You've only just tasted the freedom of God,
    you haven't yet had your fill.
Trust in the Lord who is with us today –
    you only have to be still.'

[Continued

But then the Lord said to Moses,
   'Why do my people cry out?
They know the way I've led them,
   so why do they stand and doubt?
Forget the false memories of Egypt;
   it wasn't as good as they say.
Face up to the call of the future.
Go forward! There's no other way.'
So Moses walked down to the edge of the sea;
   at God's word, he stretched out his hand.
A wind from the east blew the waters right back
   and the people went through on dry land.

To live in the past is to live with the dead,
   to be captives of things that have gone.
But tomorrow is full of the promise of God
   and today is our chance to move on.

THE TEN COMMANDMENTS
(with supplements)

Exodus 20:1-17; Deuteronomy 5:1-21

1. I am the Lord your God,
    who gave you freedom from slavery
    and brought you into being as a people.
   There is no other God. Worship only me.

   Never think that because I am the only God,
   you are the only people. I am the God of all
   peoples everywhere.

2. Do not invent lesser gods to worship,
    whether of wood or stone,
    whether objects or creatures
    whether ideas or people.
   If you turn from me to them
    you are asking for trouble,
    for I alone am the source
    of your life and well-being.

   If it helps you to try and picture me,
   remember that I am present in goodness,
   beauty and love wherever they are found.

[Continued

3. Do not take my name lightly.
   You abuse it at your cost.

   Never treat the things of the spirit with contempt.
   They are the very basis of your being.

4. Remember the day of rest;
       not only for yourself,
       but for the sake of your family,
       your colleagues, your employees,
       and the good of my creation.

   Remember also the days of work. Use them
   creatively for the good of the community and
   the health of the planet earth.

5. Respect your father and your mother,
       so that your family life may flourish.

   Nurture all the children, that they may grow strong
   in body, mind and spirit, and learn how to love.

6. Do not commit murder.

   All life is precious. Treat it with due care.

7. Do not commit adultery.

   Lifelong marriage is one of my best ideas. Do nothing to
   damage it. Do everything you can to sustain it.

8. Do not steal.

    *The wealth of the world is for the good of the
    world. Enjoy the wealth you have, but learn the
    art of giving and sharing.*

9. Do not spread evil gossip about your neighbour.

    *Speak about others, as you would like them to
    speak about you. Or say nothing at all.*

10. Do not look at your neighbour's life and possessions
    through jealous, greedy eyes.

    *Be yourself, and make the very best of what you have
    and are. Only you can do that. Value your uniqueness.*

NOT BREAD ALONE

Exodus 16:11-17:6; Deuteronomy 8:1-10

Israel in the wilderness,
    was fed by God
    with manna for her daily bread
    and quails at evening time
    for unexpected meat.

Her thirst was quenched
    with water from the rock;
    unbruised her feet,
    her clothes untorn.
For God was teaching her
    to trust his word
    and not depend for life
    on bread alone.

We also wander
    in a wilderness.
We hunger and we thirst
    for that which satisfies,
    but, spurning heavenly gifts,
    we seek for bread alone
    and clutch at golden promises
    which only prove to be
    the stomach-churning ash
    of empty lies.

Weighed down beneath our loads
    of hoarded goods,
    we stumble on towards our vision
    of the promised land.
But soon our light is spent,
    our dream turns mirage
    and our strength is drained and lost
    beneath the sand.

God, give us strength
    to brave the desert storms.
Give us your word of hope
    which stands
    when all seems lost.
God, give us light
    that shines best
    when the night is darkest.
God, give us dreams
    that do not melt away
    like morning frost.
These are our deepest needs,
    which only you can meet.
Give us the Bread of Life
    that we may eat
    and live.

OH, THAT LAND!

Exodus 3:8; Numbers 13:17-33; Deuteronomy 11:8-17; Micah 4:3, 6:8

Oh, that land!
   that beautiful land!
   flowing with milk and honey;
   a fruitful reminder of Eden,
   with vineyards and olive groves,
   figs, dates and pomegranates,
   and the spring flowers of Galilee
   garlanding the fish-abundant sea.

Oh, that land!
   that holy land!
   rich in holy history
   and abounding in holy places,
   enshrining the memory
   of holy people and their holy lives;
   always drawing
   the half-expectant feet
   of spirit-thirsty pilgrims.

Oh, that land!
   that promised land!
   birthplace of visions,
   but graveyard of prophets
   where dreams of *shalom*
   turn to nightmares of hate;
   victim of empires,
   battleground of nations,

dusty with terror
and sweating with pain.
When will the weapons
give way to the ploughshares?
When will the bitter tears
sweeten with joy?
When will Jerusalem
shine like a lantern,
not with war's fire
but with glorious peace?

And yet, in that land,
that long-bloodstained land
of flaming fanatics,
exploding assassins,
armour-plated giants
and stone-throwing boys,
thank God for those others
who bind up the wounded,
who nurture the children
and work for the peace.
For those who do justice,
those who love kindness
and those who have learned
to walk humbly with God,
they are the chosen ones,
they are God's people,
who look for the promised land
sworn by the Lord.

CLOUDS AND PROPHETS

Psalm 104:3b-4; Exodus 13:21

The clouds are like the prophets of God,
    overshadowing the land
    with warnings of bad weather.
In gloomy shades of grey
    they shut out all brightness –
    threatening storms.
They sweep relentlessly above our heads,
    and, heedless of mocking protests,
    prepare for the deluge.

The clouds are like the prophets of God,
    beautiful upon the mountains.
They pour out their life
    on the dry and dusty earth,
    promising paradise in the desert;
    and through them
    we catch visions of heaven.

For the clouds in the sky,
    like the prophets below,
    preach both warning and hope.

By a pillar of cloud
    the slaves were led to freedom,
    and from Sinai's clouds
    received the Law of God.

But shall we heed
    the cloudy prophets
    we ourselves have made –
    the toxic acid rain,
    the chemist's poisonous breath
    which damage leaf and brain
    and promise only death?
They splutter and they fume
    their messages of doom,
    and nuclear nimbus' radio-active rage
    predicts the ending of our age –
    while unseen gases eat away
    the planet's shield
    against each deadly cosmic ray.

Lord, give us ears to hear and eyes to see,
    and save us from our blind cupidity.
Alas! we have no mercy of our own;
    for that we must look up
    to you alone.

CHARIOTS OF FIRE

2 Kings 6:11-17

Elisha's servant watched
    as hostile forces gathered round
    the threatened city.
Filled with fear, he ran
    to tell the prophet,
    saying, 'Master, we are lost;
    what can we do,
    who are so few,
    against so many?'
Elisha's face showed
    neither fear nor pity
    as he answered, simply,
    'There are more with us
    than are with them.'
And, bowing low, he prayed,
    'Lord God,
    open my servant's eyes
    that he may see.'
And when the servant's eyes were opened
    he could see the hillside
    all around his master
    filled with horses
    and with chariots of fire.

Lord, in those bleak and sombre times
    when all the news we hear is bad,
    and everything that's good
    seems to be threatened
    by relentless regiments of evil;
    and when those who struggle for the right
    seem weak
    and in real danger of being overwhelmed –
Lord, in such times
    open our eyes to see
    that there are more with you
    than with your foes.

Show us the unseen power at work
    in those who love the right
    and stand for justice
    and for peace;
    whose public service,
    gentle care
    and unregarded duties
    help maintain the common good.

And when the daily benefits
    we take for granted
    are despised by those
    who only would destroy;
    give us the grace and courage
    to defend the best.
Before it is too late,
    Lord, open our blind eyes.

[Continued

And when the powers of dark
   so fill the air
   that all seems lost,
   Lord, help us to look up
   and see the stars
   still shining brightly
   in the midnight sky,
   like heavenly chariots of fire.
Open our eyes to see
   and not lose hope.

THE PROPHETS OF GOD

1 Kings 18; Amos 5:10-24; Hosea 2; Isaiah 6;
Jeremiah 31:31-34; Ezekiel 37:1-14

God's prophets are the ones who hear and see
   when all around them are both deaf and blind.
They doggedly continue to believe
   when doubt enfeebles every other mind.
The prophets of the Lord are flames of hope
   in dreary days of dark and cold despair.
They are the ones who take the side of love
   when hate and fear and cries for swift revenge,
   like ghastly demons, infiltrate the air.

In times of drought, official prophets fail
   to rouse the gods and check the nation's vice;
   but bold Elijah simply kneels in prayer
   and fire from heav'n lights up his sacrifice.

And later, when he fled the wicked queen
   and ran to distant Sinai's holy hill,
   he heard, after the wind, earthquake and fire,
   the awesome whisper of God's righteous will.

[Continued

51

When false religion dulls the people's soul,
    the poor are crushed by wealth's unfeeling hand;
    but Amos cries, 'Let streams of justice flow!'
    and warns of judgement on the stubborn land.

Hosea's love for his unfaithful wife
    led him to understand God's own deep ache
    to bind his faithless people with love's cords –
    cords which, unlike his heart, would never break.

Sad Jeremiah warned of coming doom,
    and yet he dreamed that when the worst was done
    the Lord would write a Covenant on the heart
    to replace that which had been carved in stone.

Ezekiel saw a valley full of bones,
    and thought of exiled Israel's shrivelled hope;
    but, prompted by the living word of God,
    he called on Spirit's breath to raise them up.

O Lord, when we are lost in faithless wrong
    and cannot see beyond our present pain,
    help us look up with prophets' eyes and see
    your future, full of light and hope again.

ONE DAY

Isaiah 2:4; Micah 4:3, 4; Isaiah 11:6-9;
Leviticus 25:8-12; Revelation 21:1, 4

One day
    the world will live in peace,
    for God will settle our disputes
    and we shall beat our swords to ploughs
    and turn our spears to pruning hooks;
    for nation will no longer fight
    with nation, and will learn no more
    the cruel strategies of war,
    but everyone will live secure
    and free from fear –
    one day.

One day
    the earth will be renewed,
    and harmony will reign
    among all living things;
    and wolf and lamb, leopard and goat
    shall live in peace,
    while children play
    and meet no harm
    from deadly snake
    or roaring lion;
    for none shall hurt
    and none destroy
    in all the land;

[Continued

and as the waters fill the sea
so shall the knowledge
of the Lord our God
fill all the earth –
one day.

One day
all those who live and work
like slaves
shall be set free,
debts cancelled,
land restored,
in that great triumph of the Lord,
the year of Jubilee,
when there's an end to death
and grief and pain,
when every tear is wiped away –
one day.

Let us then play our part
by getting ready for that day
with all our heart –
today.

A PROPHET IN BABYLON

Isaiah 40; Psalm 137:1-6

By what surprising grace
   did this lone prophet,
   exiled in Babylon,
   have the faith
   to see the God of Israel
   not as the defeated God
   of a defeated people,
   but as the Lord of all?

Did he not see around him
   all the glory and the grandeur
   that was Babylon –
   the wealth and splendour
   of her palaces and temples
   and the famous gardens?
Was he not impressed
   by all the pomp and dignity,
   the might and majesty
   of emperors and kings?

Did he not understand
   that God's own Jerusalem
   and holy sanctuary
   were nothing now but dust,

[Continued

while his decimated people
bowed in subjection
to a foreign law?
What miracle of faith
enabled him to see
the gods of Babylon
as painted wooden idols
wobbling on their stands,
compared to Israel's living God
whose breath shakes nations
and whose power compels the stars?

The ragged exiles
hung their harps upon the trees
and had no heart for song;
but this lone, unnamed prophet
heard the music of the Lord
in an alien land,
and could not help but sing
of God's inevitable victory –
'Take comfort from your everlasting God,
he knows your plight; he comes to take you home.
He made the world; he does not lack in power.
He gives his strength to those who tire and fall,
and those who trust and wait will rise renewed.
They'll walk and run; on eagles' wings they'll soar.
For though the grass may wither, flowers fade,
the word of God endures for evermore.'

PSALMS
AND
WISDOM

GREEN ARE THE PASTURES

Psalm 23

Green are the pastures of God's peace;
    still are the waters of his comforting.
His streams renew the springs within my heart;
    his Spirit satisfies my deepest needs.

Right are the footpaths where God leads;
    high are the mountains of his holiness.
Through darkest valleys I am not afraid;
    his presence keeps me safe along his way.

Glad is the everlasting home;
    rich is the table of God's welcoming.
My vessel overflows with God's rich wine:
    goodness and mercy now and evermore.

THE FOOLISH HEART

Psalm 14:1 and Psalm 53:1

What kind of heart is that
    which says there is no God?
Is it a heart, which is not moved
    by beauty, truth or good?
Surely it can't have seen
    the buds unfolding in the spring,
    or wild flowers dancing in the sun;
    nor watched across the bay at night
    the silver pathway of the moon.
Has it no sight, this faithless heart?

Yet even those
    who cannot see the sunlight
    still can feel its warmth.
And God, who hides in his creation,
    has a presence which,
    unseen, can still be felt
    within the heart.

[Continued

Is unbelief so cold and numb
    it cannot soften
    to the clutch of baby fingers
    round the thumb?
Has it not held a loved one's hand
    in health or sickness
    or in death?
For these alone give evidence
    of Spirit's universal breath.

Perhaps the stubborn heart
    was never moved
    to feel compassion at another's loss,
    nor yet, itself in pain or fear,
    to recognise the eager help
    of neighbour or of friend,
    or see the kindness
    in a stranger's eyes.
And has it never been inspired
    by those who,
    giving self for others,
    have revealed God's grace;
    nor ever moved by him who died
    to save the human race?
Is such a heart not even melted
    by the heat of Love's embrace?

For this proud heart
    assumes too much
    and does not think enough.
It knows the secrets of the atom,
    and the structure of the brain;
    it understands the mysteries
    of living cell and gene;
    it unravels the beginnings
    of the world of space and time –
But when it looks above
    to scan the star-filled sky,
    it takes for granted all that is,
    and never thinks to ask
    the question, 'Why?'

Oh foolish heart,
    which, saying 'No' to God,
    stares into hopeless dark;
    turn, even now,
    turn to the smallest spark of light
    and shout out 'Yes' to life.

BE STILL

Psalm 46:10; 1 Kings 19:11-12

God   Learn to be still, be still within,
            and you will know that I am God.

The People   Lord our God, how can we know you,
            how discern your righteous will,
            when your voice is drowned and silenced
            by a world that's never still?
    We are deafened by the roaring
            of our ever-rolling wheels,
            and the screaming of our music
            drowns the sigh of your appeals.
    For our minds are sore bewildered
            by the news world's ceaseless chatter,
            and our bodies are exhausted
            by life's unrelenting clatter.

God   Then be still, be still within,
            and you will know that I am God.

The People   Lord our God, how can we hear you
            through the storms of hate and pain?
    Can the whisper of your mercy
            rise above sin's hurricane?
    For our ears ring with the thunder
            of the beating drums of war,
            and the engines of Man's vengeance
            shake the earth and fill the air.

God   You can hear me, if you listen,
             with your hearts in tune with mine,
             for beneath the sounds which deafen
             lies the Spirit's secret sign.
For I speak in voiceless suffering,
             in the tears of the distressed;
             and I speak in awe full silence
             through the eyes of the oppressed.

So, be silent, all you nations,
             and be still, all humankind.
I *am* with you in the earthquake,
             in the fire and in the wind.
But my Way is love, not hatred,
             and I work with gentle power,
             in the courage and compassion
             of the servants of the poor.
And to you who learn to listen
             I will speak with words of peace.
I will be your strength and refuge,
             until wind and fire shall cease.

So be still, and you will know;
             be truly still and you will know
             that I am God.

THE PLACE OF WORSHIP

Psalm 63:1-4; Psalm 84:1-2; Psalm 122:1

We thank you, Lord most holy,
    for the place of worship in our lives,
    the hour of prayer, when we can turn
    from our own narrow self-concern
    to that which is greater
    than ourselves.

For your being is beyond our thinking,
    and your glory is beyond our imagining.
But your love is always closer
    than our feeling;
    and the riches of your Spirit
    are always within our reaching.

Without this access
    to the treasuries of heaven,
    how poor our lives would be;
    how wasted in their fruitlessness,
    without this sweet refreshment from above.
It is with parched and fainting souls we bring
    our empty vessels to the spring
    of your eternal love.

Lord, calm our stressed and anxious minds,
   which fret in busyness with many things.
Teach us to wait on you in quietness.
Forgive the dullness of our understanding –
   and our hesitant response to your good will.
Move us with the sound of sacred music.
Warm us with the company of your people.
Inspire us with the truth
   of faith's enduring story.
But, mostly,
   fill us
   with your very self;
   that on the day of reckoning
   we shall have more to offer you
   than words and rituals
   and vain achievements.

Teach us, who meet within this house,
   to make our daily lives
   places of worship, too;
   until the whole wide world
   becomes your holy Temple,
   in which all things
   gladly praise your name.

SING A NEW SONG

Psalm 96 and Psalm 98

Sing a new song to the Lord –
 not the old song of vengeance and hate,
 the raucous shout of zenophobia,
 the bitter lament of prejudice and fear,
 nor the strident cry of racial discord
 and the stiff-jawed growl
 of unrelenting power.

But let the world resound
 with the music of hope,
 and thrill to the harmonies
 of reconciliation.
Let the whole earth sing
 the soothing melody of mercy,
 until the air is filled
 with the voices of thanksgiving
 and all life beats
 to the rhythm of our God.

LIFE, BEAUTY AND LOVE

Psalm 104:24

We praise you, O God, for life –
  in every green and growing thing,
  in every swimming, creeping, running, flying creature,
  in every human being, newborn into the world,
  in every beating heart and active limb,
  in breath and movement, brain and thought –
We praise you, O God, for life.

We praise you, O God, for beauty –
  shining in light of sun and colour of flower,
  dancing in leaf and sea and skimming bird,
  singing in wind and stream and human music,
  laughing in poem and speech,
  shouting in storm and mountain,
  silent in stars and smiles and falling snow –
We praise you, O God, for beauty.

[Continued

We praise you, O God, for love –
  most of all for love –
  your love for us and our frail love for you,
  the love of man and woman, adult and child,
  the love of neighbours, colleagues and friends,
  the love of strangers, crossing divides
  the love which binds the world,
  heals wounds, cheers sorrows and restores lost hopes.
We praise you, O God, for love –
  most of all
  for love.

PHONING HOME

Psalm 130:1–6

I'm here, Lord.
Can you hear me?
I'm lost, Lord,
    in an alien world,
    like a drop-out from heaven.
I've fallen from the light
    into the darkness
    and the clouds of glory have long gone.
I'm phoning home because
    I need to hear a friendly voice,
    some reassurance, comfort, hope,
    some guidance and advice – anything.
I need to know you're still there
    and that you know I'm here,
    lonely and afraid.
Answer me, Lord.
I'm holding the receiver to my ear.
Can you hear the tone?
It's urgent, Lord.
I'm waiting, Lord.
Can't you hear it ringing,
    ringing, ringing, ringing, ringing . . .?

GOD KNOWS

Psalm 139

Lord, you know me through and through,
   every little thing I do,
   when I work and when I rest,
   when I'm happy, when depressed.
Lord, you know and understand;
   hold me in your loving hand.

Lord, you know my every word
   long before it's even heard.
You discern my thoughts and dreams,
   all my secret plans and schemes.
Lord, you know and understand;
   hold me in your loving hand.

Lord, wherever I may go,
   speeding on or moving slow,
   there I find you by my side,
   present help and constant guide.
Lord, you know and understand;
   hold me in your loving hand.

Lord, you formed me in the womb;
   wove my being on life's loom.
Great and marvellous is your art,
   far beyond all human thought.
Lord, you know and understand;
   hold me in your loving hand.

Lord, examine my poor heart;
   take away the evil part.
Lead me further, day by day,
   in your everlasting way.
Lord, you know and understand;
   hold me in your loving hand.

WHERE CAN WISDOM BE FOUND?

Job 28:12-28

Where can wisdom be found?
And where is the source of understanding?
No one knows the way to it.
It isn't to be found in the land of the living –
    not even in the letters to *The Times*,
    or the leaders in *The Daily Telegraph*;
The Sun knows nothing of it,
    and the *News of the World* has not exposed it.
We examine the files of the statisticians
    and say, 'It is not in them'.
We read the latest Government reports,
    but they do not satisfy our searching.
Fists full of dollars cannot buy it,
    nor can it be exchanged for hoards of gold.
Sotheby's haven't put it up for auction,
    nor is it offered as a quiz show prize.

Where, then, does wisdom come from?
And where is the source of understanding?
No creature on earth has seen it,
    and it is hidden from the birds of the air.
Astronauts haven't discovered it in outer space,
    and psychoanalysts have not met it
    as they plumbed the inner depths.

But God understands the way to wisdom.
He alone knows its source.
For he can see to the ends of the earth
    and surveys everything under the heavens.
When he set in place the cosmic laws,
    and balanced the forces of the universe,
    then he declared his understanding
    and revealed the wonder of his ways.
And now he says to all mankind,
    'Consider this:
    a sense of wonder is wisdom,
    and to depart from evil,
    that is understanding.'

THE ROUNDABOUT OF LIFE

Ecclesiastes 1:1–11; Revelation 21:1–5a

Life is like a roundabout,
    Ecclesiastes said.
The days and seasons come and go, and then –
    they come and go again.
For life is like a roundabout
    and like a roundabout,
    when we get off it
    we shall not be sure
    that we've done any more
    than come back where we started from.
We go to work, to earn our bread,
    to give us strength
    to rise from bed
    to go to work
    and earn our keep
    to give us strength
    to rise from sleep
    and work some more.
Is that what days are for?
Is that what life's about –
    a ride upon a roundabout?
Is that what makes life tick?
If so, like riding on a roundabout,
    no wonder that it sometimes
    makes us sick.

But stop, before you lose
    your common sense insistence,
    and begin to doubt
    that there is any meaning
    in existence.
Stop and think.

This world *is* like a roundabout.
It spins once round each day
    and yearly round the sun –
    but not for fun.
There is a purpose
    in its revolutions.
They bathe the earth
    in light and warmth,
    which make their vital contributions
    to the growth of living things.
It is not love or money
    make the world go round.
It is the world's rotations
    which make love and life
    and work and wealth
    come into being
    by the means of
    countless transmutations.
Repetition is not,
    as Ecclesiastes thought,
    a recipe for boredom and despair.
It is the catalyst of change.
It fills the air
    with promises
    of something new,
    as every generation
    builds on that which went before.

[Continued

For going round and round
    is not a static exercise;
    it is the means
    of progress and surprise,
    as those ancient ones
    were to reveal:
    the anonymous inventors
    of the wheel.

So do not give up hope.
It is the daily round
    and oft repeated task
    which make our lives
    more meaningful
    than we might dare to ask.
For we add vital contributions
    to those fruitful revolutions
    by which God is, every moment,
    making new his good creation.
Don't depair while you've the chance
    to join in God's creative dance;
    but give instead a joyful shout
    because you're here to take a ride
    on life's fantastic roundabout.

GOD'S GOOD TIME

Ecclesiastes 3

Our measurements of time are based upon
　　the movements of the earth, the moon, the sun;
　　to which we add the seconds, minutes, hours –
　　inventions of ingenious human powers.

We capture time, we think, in silver clocks,
　　and bind it up in diaries with brass locks.
We live by schedule and timetabled slot,
　　which make us feel in charge – but we are not.

For this is techno-time, mechanical,
　　relentless, callous and tyrannical.
It marks the passing days and months and years
　　with cold precision in its cogs and gears;
　　a meter ticking over, as we drive
　　towards a deadline we will not survive.

But such a view of time is an illusion,
　　and leads us surely to the wrong conclusion.
For time is not a rigid iron cage,
　　imprisoning every predetermined age.
It is the space in which we live and grow,
　　the mystic ocean in which all things flow;
　　the loom where weaves an awesome tapestry,
　　each day a bar in God's eternal symphony.

THE CANDLE

Proverbs 20:27 (AV); Matthew 5:14-16; 10:39

The candle in the window
    shines out into the world.
But as it shines
    it slowly burns away;
    it can do no other.
In giving its light
    it gives its very self,
    gradually becoming less and less
    as the wax and the wick burn down,
    until they are nothing at all.

But the light from the candle
    goes on shining still,
    as it travels out and out
    into the universe –
    beyond the earth,
    the moon and the stars
    to the very edges of creation.
And even then it goes on shining
    into all eternity.

And that light
    is the very soul of the candle –
    not the wax or the wick,
    but the light.
But when the wax and the wick have gone,
    the candle's light lives on
    still giving glory to God.

JESUS
AND
HIS FOLLOWERS

SUPERSTAR

Matthew 1:18a

You should have been born in this century, Lord.
We'd have treated you better today,
     with NHS doctors and midwives on hand
     instead of a stable and hay;
     and government handouts to help you along,
     and state education from one.
You'd have no need to learn your dad's carpenter's trade,
     when a student life offers such fun.

You should have been born in this century, Lord;
     we'd have been quick to see your real worth.
Your words about lilies and birds in the air
     would have suited the Friends of the Earth.
And your wandering lifestyle and sandals and beard
     would have won you a following band
     from the midsummer travellers on Salisbury Plain
     or the squatters on derelict land.

Your miraculous cures would have caused quite a stir,
     and you'd soon have become quite well known,
     with a spot on a chat show, a clip in the News
     and an article in *Woman's Own*.
You should have been born in this century, Lord,
     because PR is one of our arts:
     you'd have written a series of best-selling books
     and even got hits in the charts.

You could then have set out for the lights of New York
   and a lecture tour all round the States.
They'd be sure to invite you on *This Is Your Life,*
   and treat you as one of the greats.
You should have been born in this century, Lord;
   the people need stars to adore,
   and the worst that could happen is death by neglect
   'cause we don't have the cross any more.
And, even today, resurrection can come,
   though admittedly not quite the same:
   it consists of a musical show of your life
   on the Broadway that leads to true fame.

So you'd have survived to live on to old age
   and have died on a hospital bed.
And we'd smile to ourselves with a nostalgic smile,
   when we heard what the newsreader said:
   about how you'd been famous in days long gone by,
   and in fact you'd been quite a trendsetter.
You should have been born in this century, Lord,
   or was crucifixion much better?

NUNC DIMITTIS

Luke 2:25-32

Now, Lord, please let your servant go in peace.
Your ancient promise is at last fulfilled.
My eyes have seen salvation in this child,
    whom you have sent in love for all mankind.
His light reveals your truth in every land.
The brightest gem in Israel's crown is he.
His love will move the heart of all the world,
    until his Spirit fills earth, sky and sea.

ENOUGH

Matthew 14:15-21; Mark 6:35-44; Luke 9:12-17; John 6:5-13

When Jesus asked his friends
    to feed the hungry crowd
    they said,
    'It's far too late today;
    we can't afford to pay;
    let's send them all away
    to feed themselves.'

But Jesus answered,
    'No. You will not need a lot.
    Find out how much you've got.'

They came again to him and said,
    'We've only found two fish
    and these five loaves of bread;
    but what's the use of them
    among so many?'

Jesus replied,
    'It is enough. You need
    no more than this to feed
    these hungry people.'

However big your task,
    if only you will ask
    you're sure to find enough –
    enough to start with.

[Continued

They gave him what they had
   and he looked up to heaven,
   giving thanks to God.
And then he told his friends
   to share the food
   among the people
   sitting on the ground;
   and that's when,
   to their great surprise,
   they found there was enough
   to go around.

However big your task,
   if only you will ask,
   God will provide enough
   to go along with.

After the people had been fed,
   the friends of Jesus
   picked up all the pieces
   of the fish and bread
   that were left over,
   so that nothing
   should be wasted,
   and they filled
   twelve baskets
   with food
   that people
   had not even tasted.

However big your task,
   if only you will ask,
   you'll have more than enough
   when it is finished.

THE LAW OF CHRIST

Matthew 5-7

The Law of Christ,
    like the Law of Moses,
    comes down from the mountains.
It is our guide
    to take us climbing
    to perfection.
It descends from the hills
    to the people of the valley,
    and speaks seditiously
    of a higher life.

It speaks to the banker
    of treasure in heaven;
    of turning the cheek
    to the hard-bitten fighter;
    of praying in secret
    to the egotist preacher;
    of a plain 'yes' or 'no'
    to the sly politician;
    and of flowers in the field
    neither toiling nor spinning,
    and of not being anxious
    for food, drink and clothing
    to the business tycoon
    and voracious consumer;
    of love and forgiveness

[Continued

and lending and giving;
of the lust and the anger
in everyone living.

So speaks Christ's Law
to all those who will hear.
But the way that he shows us
is long, hard and narrow,
and appears uninviting
to those who, seduced by
the voice of false prophets,
have learned to make light
of the truth, and make dark of
the light.

Thank God for the lowly,
the restless and downcast,
who lift up their eyes
to the hills where their help is,
and reach for the heights
of the Spirit of love.
Lord, move us to follow,
in spite of the hardship,
that even our poor lives,
so worn by the journey,
may shine with your light
from the mountains above.

THE LORD'S PRAYER

Matthew 6:9-13

Eternal God, our truest Friend,
    may joyful praises never end
    in honour of your name.
Your reign begin within our hearts
    and reach to earth's remotest parts
    with ever-spreading fame.
Your will be done, your dream come true,
    when all creation is made new
    in love's refining flame.

Give us, meanwhile, our daily bread,
    enough for body, heart and head,
    enough to see us through.
As we forgive another's debt
    and even manage to forget,
    so pardon our debts too.
Protect us from temptation's lies,
    so that, unfooled by sin's disguise,
    we'll walk in peace with you.

Yours is the kingdom, yours the might.
Yours is the splendour of the light.
Yours is the everlasting right.
Yes! Lord, and yes! again.

MARTHA

Luke 10:38-42; Matthew 11:28

While Mary sat in quietness
   at the Master's feet,
   Martha fussed and sweated
   in the kitchen's heat.
She was too busy doing
   what she thought was good.
She had no time to rest a while
   and listen to the Lord.
Giving and doing
   were Martha's chosen role,
   which helped her to think
   that she was in control.
Yet, in her care-filled bustling
   she had found
   no real tranquillity –
   a gift that only comes
   to those who learn
   how to receive and be.

For Martha's God
   is god of hearth and home –
   house-trained, domestic.
She does not know
   the living God,
   whose energy
   drives all of heaven and earth –
   awesome, majestic.
Nor does she hear,
   within her anxious breast,
   his gentle word
   to all who labour
   and are heavy laden:
   'Come to me,
   and I will give you rest.'

SITTING BY THE EDGE OF THE POOL

John 5:1-15

I was once content
    just staring at the waters,
    sitting by the edge of the pool;
    waiting for an angel
    to stir up the water,
    sitting by the edge of the pool.

But Jesus came
    with a word that pierced my heart;
    he asked me a question
    that tore my soul apart:
    'Do you want to be whole?'
Did I really, really want to be whole?

I was once resigned
    to a life without a purpose,
    sitting by the edge of the pool;
    with a paralysed mind
    that didn't need a purpose,
    sitting by the edge of the pool.

Then Jesus came
    and got me off my seat;
    he challenged me to stand
    on my own feet:
    'Pick up your mat and walk!' –
    and I did, oh yes I did!
And then I knew, within my soul,
    he'd made me whole!

THE WIDOW'S GIFT

Mark 12:41-44; Luke 21:1-4

When Jesus saw the widow
    put her coins in the treasury,
    he was impressed –
    enough to point her out
    to his disciples
    as someone who knew
    what giving meant.

The first thing that he noticed
    when he saw her in the Temple
    was the startling smallness
    of her gift –
    two coins worth very little,
    lost under the weight
    of much larger offerings.
Yet she didn't ask herself,
    as we might ask ourselves –
'What is the use of an offering so small?'
And she didn't excuse herself,
    as we might excuse ourselves,
    by saying, 'What difference
    can so little make?'
She just gave what she had,
    with no questions asked;
    and Jesus, unknown to her,
    noticed it.

But though he was impressed
    by the smallness of her gift,
    what really moved him
    was the greatness of her giving.
She gave everything she had.
She only had two coins,
    but gave them both.
If she'd been sensible,
    she could have kept one at least
    for her own needs,
    which were far greater
    than the needs of the Temple,
    but recklessly she gave them both.
She took the great commandment
    at its face value,
    and loved God with all she had.
When Jesus saw
    that she had given everything
    to God,
    he was moved, and inspired;
    and I like to think
    that, later, when he
    broke the bread and poured the wine
    as symbols of his own self-giving,
    he remembered
    the poor widow's gift.

KING JESUS

John 18:33-37

They sometimes say that Jesus was a King,
    and yet he had no throne or golden crown,
    no royal robes or jewelled ring.
He had no army to enforce his Law;
    his wealth was not in palaces or lands;
    he lived his life among the poor.

But King he is; and though he reigns unseen,
    and love's the only power at his command –
    in truth, no greater King has ever been.

HUMBLE ACCESS

Matthew 26:26-28; John 6:55-57

Lord, we come to this your table
    trusting in your love alone,
    hoping in your mercy, for we
    have no goodness of our own.

Yet you do not give us only
    crumbs, which from your table fall;
    you provide that bread and wine, which
    is the richest food of all.

Broken bread and broken body,
    poured out wine and blood you give;
    we in you and you in us, Lord,
    by this grace for ever live.

JESUS CAME TO SAVE US

John 13:1-5; Mark 14:22-25; Luke 22:39-44;
Matthew 26:57-68; John 18:28-19:16; Mark 15:29-32;
Acts 10:39b; John 19:38-42; Luke 24:1-12

Room prepared; disciples meet;
Bowl and towel; washing feet;
God's plan ready to complete –
    Jesus came to save us.

Broken bread and poured out wine;
Holy body, blood divine;
Was there ever food so fine? –
    Jesus came to save us.

Midnight garden, olive wood,
Prayers of anguish, sweat like blood;
He accepts the will of God –
    Jesus came to save us.

Priestly pride and Roman power;
Soldiers' lash; spectators' jeer;
Now has come his finest hour –
    Jesus came to save us.

Wounded flesh and flowing blood;
Sharp the nails and rough the wood;
He reveals the love of God –
    Jesus came to save us.

Linen cloth and borrowed tomb;
Spices mask the smell of doom;
Earth can give him no more room –
    Jesus came to save us.

Empty grave, angelic light;
Friends bewildered by the sight;
He has ended death's dark night –
    Jesus came to save us.

STONES

Matthew 28:2

Beware of stones;
   they can be dangerous.

Some stones can trip,
   and the unwary,
   surprised in their carefree path
   by unexpected stumbling blocks
   fall, and are broken.

Others, more careful,
   walk around the stones,
   but with eyes only for obstacles –
   they are blind
   to a wider vision.

Others pick up their stones
   and strain beneath the weight
   of guilt and fear;
   grim Atlases,
   bearing the world's burdens
   on their neurotic shoulders.

But some kick stones,
   like laughing schoolboys
   oblivious of the risk, until,
   too late, the damage has been done.

Or stones are thrown from angry fists
    against the unyielding armour of authority,
    or the stubborn heads of nonconformists,
    or the easy target of the vulnerable,
    or the innocent bystander.

Some bravely build with stones,
    but their unsteady efforts
    do not always stand the test
    of quakes and storms.

Such are the various tricks
    which we have learned
    in handling stones,
    and each one troublesome.

God has a better way –
    his Easter morning angel came
    and rolled away the stone
    that blocked Christ's tomb;
    and sat on it.

PRISONER

Romans 7:14–8:2

I am a prisoner in Space,
    locked in a physical capsule
    of body and brain;
    reaching out five sensual arms
    with cosmic longing,
    but grasping little.

I am a prisoner in Time,
    always losing my bright future
    in a disappointing past,
    and sooner or later conceding
    that my brief appearance is ending
    to relieved applause.

I am a prisoner of Life,
    bound by the clockwork demands
    of the daily schedule;
    systematically drained
    by relentless routine
    and timetabled triviality.

But, worst of all,
    I am a prisoner of Self,
    whose dreams are quenched
    by the inner nightmare
    of intrinsic defects,
    climbing the down escalator
    with persistent gravity.

Who, then, will come,
    to release the captive,
    declaring the year of Jubilee?
Thank God for Christ,
    Master of Space, Time and Life,
    who captures my Self
    and sets me free.

IN GOD'S GARDEN

1 Corinthians 3:9 (REB)

Though I have known from early childhood that many tiny flowerets grow in our dear Lord's garden, it is only recently that I started to compile a list of them. Here are a few possible varieties.

Suburbiana Respectabilia

This respectable climber
    grows well
    in pleasant conditions
    and with the help
    of a suitable
    adjacent building.
Plant in September
    and it will blossom at Christmas
    and, with sufficient care,
    bear fruit by Easter.
Then it rests until Autumn.
It does not easily
    survive transplanting.

Grandioso Ritualis

This dressy plant,
    which flourishes, surprisingly,
    in a smoky atmosphere,
    produces flowers of different colours
    for every season of the year.
It is at its best in clusters,
    which enhance its stately presence;
    and its solemn dignity
    will grace any occasion.

Hierarchico Administrasis

This pot plant flourishes behind glass,
    especially office windows,
    where it proliferates
    with minimum attention
    or encouragement.
The main problem is
    to keep its growth
    within reasonable bounds.
It bears an abundance
    of papery fruit
    all year round,
    most of which is
    entirely lacking
    in nutritional value.

[Continued

Pentecosto Dramaticalis

An extremely colourful plant,
   growing equally well
   in inner cities
   or isolated rural plots,
   and is also found
   in suburban gardens.
Its branches wave wildly
   in even the smallest breeze,
   making uncanny noises.
Its fruit is bright and tasty,
   and is said to have healing powers,
   though it can produce
   hallucinations.

Pomposa Verbosis

This impressive plant
   prefers a high location
   in full light.
It tends to dominate the garden
   and though its flowers
   can be attractive,
   its fruit can be disappointing.

Mystico Solitaris

This stark, cactus-like plant
   grows well in desert conditions –
   the more severe the conditions
   the more fragrant the flowers.
Its fruit is only valued
   by those who are lost
   in the wilderness.
To others, it has a bitter taste.

Saint

A humble plant
    which grows in any situation,
    and has been found hidden
    among all the plants
    described above.
Its simple beauty
    has the strange effect
    of bringing out the best
    in those around it,
    and its sweet aroma
    fills the air with a sense
    of calm and goodwill.

THE FRUIT OF THE SPIRIT

Galatians 5:22-23

Holy Spirit, move within us
  that we may grow in grace
  and bear good fruit.

Forgive us, Lord, when we are ruled too much by self-concern,
  and not enough by real concern for others.

May the fruit of love grow in our lives.

Forgive us, Lord, when bitterness and cynicism poison
  our hearts and distort our thinking.

May the fruit of joy grow in our lives.

Forgive us when we knowingly cause trouble and offence
  by our hurtful words and deeds.

May the fruit of peace grow in our lives.

Forgive us when we are irritable and impatient
  and in too much of a hurry.

May the fruit of patience grow in our lives.

Forgive us, Lord, for not seeing when someone
is in need of help, or for being reluctant to give it.

May the fruit of kindness grow in our lives.

Forgive us for preferring darkness to light
by nurturing pride, jealousy, dishonesty and greed.

May the fruit of goodness grow in our lives.

Forgive us when we are too ready to give up,
or unwilling to stand up for what we know is right.

May the fruit of faithfulness grow in our lives.

Forgive us when we are loud and aggressive,
bad tempered and rude.

May the fruit of gentleness grow in our lives.

Forgive us for venting our foulest feelings,
expressing our nastiest thoughts and giving way
to our worst desires.

May the fruit of self-control grow in our lives.

Holy Spirit, move within us,
that we may grow in grace
and bear good fruit. Amen.

THE CONVERTED CHURCH

Psalm 24:1

They've converted our church
    into a car showroom.
Jesus has been driven from his Temple
    by the moneychangers
    and car salesmen.
But the children of mammon
    have proved more skilled
    in attracting the eye
    of the passer-by
    than the children of light;
    for the flashing neon
    is more appealing
    than the peeling noticeboard.
The grimy stained-glass angels
    have returned to heaven
    and this worldly Temple
    is now filled
    with gleaming, metallic chariots
    promising power, freedom and delight.
The sticky brown pews,
    rigidly going nowhere,
    have been replaced
    by the luxurious leather
    of long-distance limousines;

and all those sleepy sermons
have given way
to the restrained excitement
of solemn sales talk;
while the refurbished vestry
bears hushed witness
to the ritual signing
of new covenants,
opening the road
to a mechanical promised land
by easy payments.
The old harmonium's drone
has been silenced
by the subtle murmur
of piped music;
and glossy brochures,
not brown-leaved hymnals,
sing the praises
of god the machine.

Yet over the entrance,
indelibly carved in stone,
these words can still be read –
The earth is the Lord's,
and the fullness thereof;
the world,
and they that dwell therein.

NORTH HINKSEY VILLAGE CHURCH

Luke 24:5

At first it seems just like a pretty cottage,
    with its mossy roof and warm stone walls,
    its leaded windows and its ancient peace.

Yet what strange house *is* this?
Set in a garden of leaning stones,
    the worn-out memorials of the dead,
    gravely it stands, a larger tomb
    entered by creaking doors
    of worm-filled oak;
    and inside are shadows
    and a chilling air,
    and marble skulls,
    and images of a dying man.
Could it be that this whitewashed place
    is none other than
    the sepulchre of Christ?

Its emptiness
    is like a hollow vacuum
    sealed from the passing
    traffic of the world;
    a pool of stillness
    at the centre of the whirlwind;
    a silence
    to be broken
    only by the ritual echoes
    of Sunday worship.

And as I stand at the entrance
    I can almost hear
    the message of the Easter angel –
    'Why do you seek the living
    among the dead?
    He is not here.
    He is risen.'

Yet even though I know
    he can't be buried
    in this holy shrine,
    I swear he is still present
    in his living Spirit.

A PRAYER TO THE TRINITY

Ephesians 1:16-17 (GNB, NIV); Jude 20b-21

Our Father, we sing of your wisdom and power,
    which brought into being the star and the flower.
We praise you for sunlight, for mountains and seas,
    for snow in the winter and soft summer breeze;
    for touch, taste and fragrance, for sight and for sound;
    for places of reverence where beauty is found;
    for life in its richness, its goodness and worth;
    for our wonderful home on this green planet earth.
But mostly we praise you for light from above,
    for glimpses of truth, intimations of love;
    for strength in the battle and courage to win;
    for visions of hope and forgiveness of sin.

We praise you, Christ Jesus, our Saviour and Lord,
    for the light of your story, the power of your word;
    for the things that you did and the truths that you taught;
    for the life that you lived and the love that you brought;
    for the healing, forgiveness and hope that you gave,
    when you hung on the cross, when you rose from the grave.

All praise to you, Spirit of power and of life,
    who call us from failure and weakness and strife
    to enter the kingdom of love, joy and peace.
You give us the courage and inner release
    to live for the values we read in the word
    and put into practice the truths we have heard.

Praise to our Father and Creator;
Praise to Jesus Christ our Saviour;
Praise to the Spirit our strong Helper;
Praise to our God for evermore. Amen.

THE BANK OF HEAVEN

Matthew 6:19-21; Luke 12:33-34; Romans 14:12

If you ever get to heaven,
    you'll be shown around
    by a guardian angel.
And one of the places you'll visit
    on the very first day
    will be the Celestial Bank.
(I know there *is* a bank,
    because Jesus told us
    to lay up treasures for ourselves
    in heaven.)
So they'll bring out your account,
    and with a frown and a sigh
    and a shaking of the head
    they'll probably say,
'If only you'd put more in
    on earth,
    you could have taken more out
    in heaven.'

So be warned –
    it isn't yet too late
    to start investing.

THE HOLY CITY

Revelation 21:2, 9-27; 22:1-15; Hebrews 11:10, 16b

What a surprise to find –
 after believing for years
 that heaven was like a garden,
 a green and fruitful paradise
 of peace and beauty,
 or like a palmy South Sea island
 lapped by deep blue waters
 on a beach of silver sand –
 what a surprise to find,
 that when, at the end of the Bible
 a piece of heaven
 comes floating down to earth,
 it isn't a garden at all,
 but a City.

And with its gates of pearl
 and its streets of gold
 it seems not unlike
 Las Vegas;
 except for its size.
It is a giant cube,
 one thousand five hundred miles square,
 and one thousand five hundred miles high.
It would seem to be
 a planning error
 of enormous proportions.

[Continued

115

This *Holy City*, as it's called
    (surely a contradiction in terms),
    has brought heaven
    down to earth
    with a bump.

But should we be so surprised?
Does God really want us
    to dream our destiny away
    in a soporific garden,
    (or on a pacific beach)
    where nothing happens
    for all eternity?
For our idea of heaven
    often seems to be
    a place of self-indulgence,
    and never-ending rest.
But in cities
    we have to learn how to live
    with other people,
    in an environment
    that's rarely still,
    and where there is always
    something worthwhile
    to do.

For every one of our cities
    (even Las Vegas)
    is some kind of botched attempt
    at civilisation,
    and this vision
    of the Holy City
    is God's way of saying
    that he wants civilisation too.

Gardens are wonderful
    in their place,
    and what better place for a garden
    than in a Holy City?

SCRIPTURAL INDEX

OLD TESTAMENT

Genesis
1:1-3	12
1:1-2:3	14
1:3	17
1:26-27	19
4:1-16	21
6:5-9:17	23
11:1-9	26
12:1-9	27
28:10-22	28
32:22-32	28
37:1-36	30
39:1-47:31	30

Exodus
3:1-12	34
3:2	35
3:8	44
13:21	46
14:10-16	37
16:11-17:6	42
20:1-17	39

Leviticus
25:8-12	53

Numbers
13:17-33	44

Deuteronomy
5:1-21	39
8:1-10	42
11:8-17	44

1 Kings
18	51
19:11-12	62

2 Kings
6:11-17	48

Job
28:12-28	72

Psalms
14:1	59
23	58
24:1	108
46:10	62
53:1	59
63:1-4	64
84:1-2	64
96	66
98	66
104:3b-4	46
104:24	67
122:1	64
130:1-6	69
137:1-6	55
139	70

Proverbs
20:27	78

Ecclesiastes
1:1-11	74
3	77

Isaiah
2:4	53
6	51
11:6-9	53
40	55

Jeremiah
31:31-34	51

Ezekiel
37:1-14	51

Amos
5:10-24	51

Hosea
2	51

Micah
4:3, 4	44, 53
6:8	44

NEW TESTAMENT

Matthew

1:18a	80
5-7	85
5:1-48	85
5:14-16	78
6:1-34	85
6:9-13	87
6:19-21	114
7:1-29	85
10:39	78
11:28	88
14:15-21	83
26:26-28	95
26:57-68	96
28:2	98

Mark

6:35-44	83
12:41-44	92
14:22-25	96
15:29-32	96

Luke

2:25-32	82
9:12-17	83
10:38-42	88
12:33-34	114
21:1-4	92
22:39-44	96
24:5	110
24:1-12	96

John

5:1-15	90
6:5-13	83
6:55-57	95
13:1-5	96
18:33-37	94
18:28-19:16	96
19:38-42	96

Acts

10:39b	96

Romans

7:14-8:2	100
14:12	114

1 Corinthians

3:9	102

Galatians

5:22-23	106

Ephesians

1:16-17	112

Hebrews

11:8-10, 13-16	27
11:10, 16b	115

1 John

2:16, 17	35

Jude

20b-21	112

Revelation

21:1, 4	53
21:1-5a	74
21:2, 9-27	115
22:1-15	115